TAKE CHARGE OF YOUR JOB SEARCH!

A HANDBOOK TO EMPOWER UNEMPLOYED PEOPLE TO FIND THEIR OWN JOBS

FRANCES CURIEL

Training Resource Network, Inc. ◆ St. Augustine, Florida

First Edition

Printed in the United States of America by BookCrafters.

Published by Training Resource Network, Inc., PO Box 439,
St. Augustine, FL 32085-0439.

Library of Congress Cataloging-in-Publication Data

Curiel, Frances, date.
    Take charge of your job search! : a handbook to empower unem-
ployed people to find their own jobs / Frances Curiel. -- 1st ed.
       p.   cm.
   ISBN 1-883302-11-0 (pbk.)
   1. Job hunting. I. Title
HF5382.7.C87 1997
650. 14--DC21

                96-30051
                CIP

CONTENTS

FOREWORD

THIS BOOK IS A GEM

 What is job development anyway? Is it sales? Is it about marketing? Is it job placement? Is it a skill? Is it a profession? One needs only to spend time with Frances Curiel to see that, yes, it includes all those things.

But more importantly, Frances views job development as a true art. Where others may see it as a tough, low-reward, full-of-rejection type of activity, Frances sees it as an avenue to meet a challenge head on – with creativity and energy.

As Frances would say, it's not just a matter of getting people jobs. It's about helping people to discover opportunities – opportunities to find out good things about themselves they never knew, opportunities to form new friendships, opportunities to be a part of a larger community, and opportunities to develop and use their talents.

If you want to find employment, Frances is the one to help you. Her track record is simply astonishing. If you are a job seeker with particular barriers, Frances says let's be innovative, let's look at capitalizing on the strengths you have, and let's get creative about finding solutions. If you want to work, let's go to it!

This book is a gem. Why do we think so?

It is a gem because:
- ◆ it comes straight from the heart of a real live, highly successful person who believes job development is a bona fide profession. And her career mission is to elevate it to a point where it is viewed by other professions as "right up there" with such honorable fields as medicine, business, and law. After all, assisting someone in finding meaningful work changes lives.

It is a gem because:

◆ it focuses on what people have to offer employers. And since we have two major customers – job seekers and employers – it is critical that we clearly know what valuable resources we are representing to the business community.

Frances knows how to initiate and build strong partnerships with business people. In our work with the Marriott Foundation for People with Disabilities and TransCen, Inc., we have used and practiced many of the strategies Frances proposes and we have benefited greatly. Frances believes that her job is done only when all parties are happy with the services and the outcomes they received from her. Isn't that what good working relationships are about, after all?

It is a gem because:

◆ it can be effectively used *right now*. The ideas and activities don't need to be studied – they only need to be used. As our first grade teachers told us: Practice makes perfect. We think this is a book that makes perfect sense.

Enjoy! We wish you lots of success in finding wonderful employment (and life!) opportunities through your work. And be sure to let Frances know how the book has helped you. She believes that part of professionalizing our work is the sharing of thoughts and ideas.

Lorraine Wilson
National Project Director
Bridges...from school to work
Marriott Foundation for
People with Disabilities

George Tilson, Jr., Ed. D.
Senior Vice President
TransCen, Inc.

PREFACE

This handbook was developed after providing job-seeking assistance to individuals who had been absent from the work force for an extended period of time. I have worked as a job developer with job seekers in vocational rehabilitation, in federally funded programs, and with a wide range of unemployed individuals.

In all those years, I found that after they received all available job leads and underwent employment interviews, job seekers still were unable to get the jobs they wanted. I have come to realize that even though direct job placement services were provided to these job seekers, they remained untrained in seeking employment independently. They were lacking job-seeking skills themselves.

Job seekers, in today's labor market, are more vulnerable to job change, and need to be permanently equipped with job-seeking skills. The process of developing their skills can promote self-sufficiency and independence. Yet job seekers with disabilities and other challenges are not being trained in job-seeking skills to contribute to their own independence.

Direct job placement has been a "Band-Aid" solution. If the objective is to assist job seekers in becoming self-sufficient, they must develop a lifelong skill and participate in their own job searches.

It also became apparent while I was teaching job-seeking skills that participants did not want another detailed clinical job-search handbook. They wanted a "quick, to-the-point, all-you-need, and what-has-proven-to-work-for-others" handbook.

What I found in working with unemployed people is that they almost all had one thing in common: They were in a state of stress and urgency. So, I put together what people needed to get the job they wanted, keeping it simple and filled with what works. I focus on teaching the dos, forgetting the don'ts. Why fill people with any hint of negativity? I want to create and offer a positive approach from beginning to end.

Keeping this handbook straightforward, encouraging the job seeker's participation, and maintaining a positive mode throughout the handbook has proven to be very effective in many a job seeker's efforts to find employment with which they are happy.

This book will enable job seekers to identify and locate employment opportunities that they want.

ACKNOWLEDGMENTS

I would first like to give recognition and thanks to outstanding employers who gave me the opportunity to job match and be successful in job searches: James Herold, Bank of America; Armand Paez, United Parcel Service; Robert Dictor and Eric Quarels, Marriott International; Audrianne Adams, Epson America; and Jose Uribe, Chief Auto Parts.

In addition, I would like to thank Armand Paez, United Parcel Service, and Robert Walden, Wilbur Curtis Co., for assisting me in initiating a mentoring program for youth with disabilities, which has proven to be very successful in training interns.

A thank you with deep affection to Lorraine Wilson, my friend, mentor, and editor. Without her support, belief, and determination this handbook never would had been presented for publication. She so generously gave countless hours and energy in making my dream a reality.

With highest respect and admiration, I would also like to thank George Tilson and Rich Luecking, of TransCen Inc., and Mark Donovan of the Marriott Foundation, for recognizing my work as worthy of publishing.

A special thanks to Russell Ung, Los Angeles Unified School District, and the career and transition counselors who are true advocates of the "Bridges...from school to work" project: Ray Hyde, Jerry Zwick, Lisa Raffaeli, Mike Vincent, and Chuck Trudeau. I also would like to extend my gratitude to Louis Mestas, State of California Department of Rehabilitation, and Andrew Melendrez of Innovative Rehabilitation Services.

More personally, I would like to blow a kiss to my sons Orlando, Tony, and Roland for their support and encouragement, and for their understanding of my passion and dedication for job development and the desire to be of service to others. Most importantly I thank my mother, Gloria, a special education teacher who made a difference in my life as well as countless other children.

I am grateful forever to all the job seekers I've had the opportunity to assist in their job searches. While motivating them, I was in turn motivated to assist them in getting the jobs they wanted. While they made their own personal discoveries, I too was making my own ... for I was given a gift – the gift of the opportunity to assist others in seeing their talents – and for this I am most grateful.

TAKE CHARGE OF YOUR JOB SEARCH!

A HANDBOOK TO EMPOWER UNEMPLOYED PEOPLE TO FIND THEIR OWN JOBS

INTRODUCTION

 The first question asked by people looking for jobs who come to me for assistance is:

"Do I have to memorize a lot of things?"

The answer is no! Just become familiar with the ideas in this handbook.

How you feel about each job and place of work is how you will interact with those businesses during your job search. Every interview is also different. Your answers will change most of the time, depending on circumstances. So it is best not to try to memorize a script.

I focus on teaching the dos, and not worrying too much about the don'ts. I want to create and offer a positive approach from beginning to end.

This book will enable you to identify and locate employment opportunities that you want.

WHY FIND YOUR OWN JOB?

KEYS TO FINDING YOUR OWN JOB

A successful experience job searching will promote higher self-esteem, leaving you feeling confident and motivated.

Motivation is the beginning of a cycle:

Motivation develops while learning job seeking skills. As a motivated job seeker, you'll want to do more.

Action happens as you participate in the job search.

Self-Esteem builds through performing job-seeking skills. You will feel good about yourself for getting things accomplished.

You then will work harder at your job search. This cycle will continue until you find the job you want.

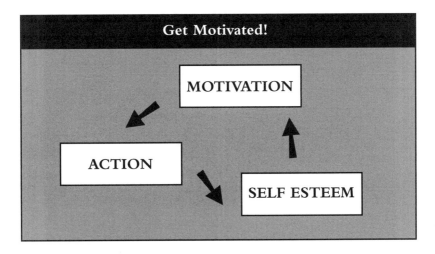

Learning by Doing

Learning how to find a job involves many skills, such as talking to employers, developing your presentation, setting up interviews, and following up on your contacts.

Participation

Participating actively will give you a sense of responsibility for your own job search.

Urgency

You develop a sense of urgency in your job search by not wasting time. You want and need a job now!

Life-Long Learning

A lifelong skill is obtained simply by knowing how to present yourself through job-seeking skills.

Job-Seeking Skills Promote:

◆ Motivation   ◆ Participation

◆ Self-Esteem   ◆ Sense of Urgency

◆ Action   ◆ Life-Long Learning

◆ Learning by Doing   *These will lead to self-sufficiency.*

There are other benefits when you participate in your own job search:

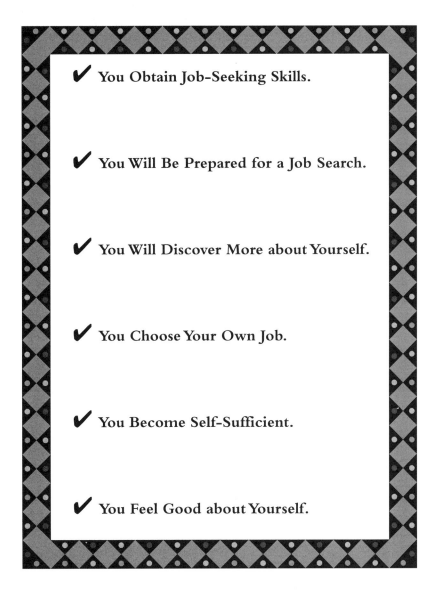

✔ **You Obtain Job–Seeking Skills.**

✔ **You Will Be Prepared for a Job Search.**

✔ **You Will Discover More about Yourself.**

✔ **You Choose Your Own Job.**

✔ **You Become Self-Sufficient.**

✔ **You Feel Good about Yourself.**

WHEN YOU ARE HANDED A JOB...

All you get is:

A

JOB

It seems the only time people think about JOBS is when they don't have one. Then the question comes up, "How can I find a job?"

With the job-seeking skills this handbook will teach you, you will have an answer.

WHEN YOU CAN FIND YOUR OWN JOB...

You have more than just a job.

You will have a lifelong skill of finding new and better jobs.

DISCOVERING YOUR TALENTS AND INTERESTS

WHO ARE YOU?

YOUR FAMILY:

Draw, write, or place pictures in the separate squares of members of your family, including pets. If you are not an artist, draw stick people.

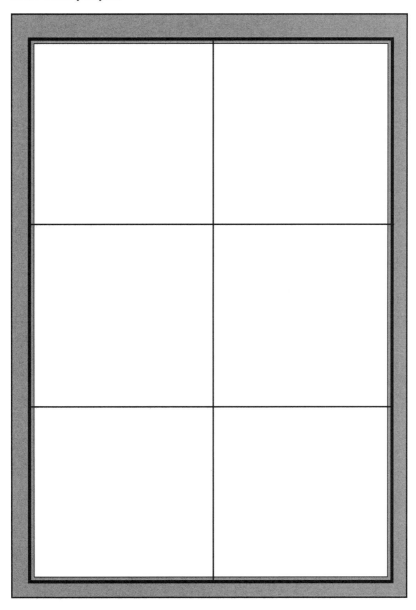

THINGS YOU LIKE:

List, place pictures, or draw things you enjoy.

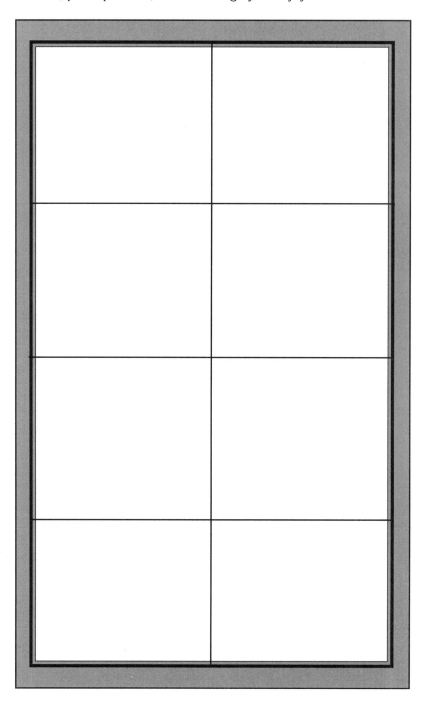

THINGS YOU ARE GOOD AT:

List, place pictures, or draw things you do well.

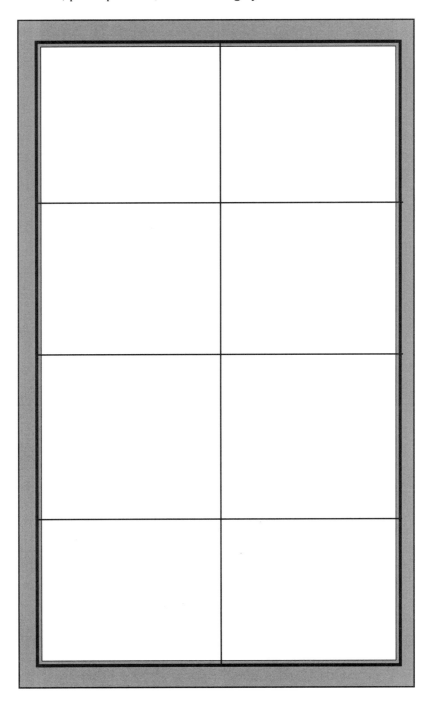

TWO ACCOMPLISHMENTS:

Write about, draw, or paste a picture of at least two of your accomplishments.

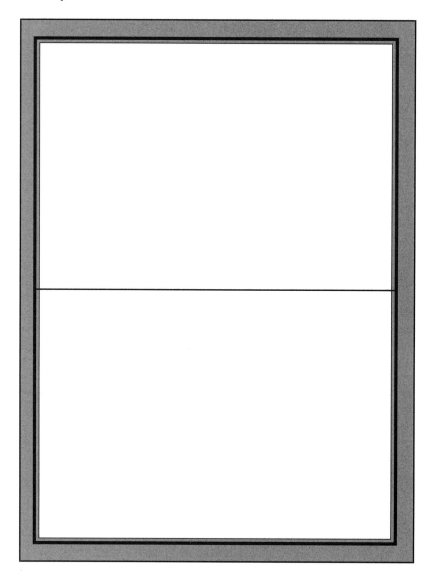

Share your completed sheets with friends. People really can get to know more about you if you share openly. By doing this, you will get to know yourself and be better able to sell yourself to an employer.

WHAT OTHERS VALUE IN YOU

Review these pages to remember how other people perceive your great personality and skills whenever you are feeling down about your job search.

Ask your friends to write: **positive personal qualities, personality traits, or job skills that describe you!**
My name is: [   ]

A) What [   ] does well is:

[   ]

B) What I like most about [   ] is:

[   ]

C) I feel [   ]'s most outstanding personal quality is:

[   ]

D) I feel [   ]'s most outstanding and attractive physical feature is:

[   ]

E) The good things others say about [   ] are:

[   ]

AUTOGRAPH PAGE

Have some fun! Ask some friends and relatives to write what they think you are good at and what they like most about you. Ask them to sign their note.

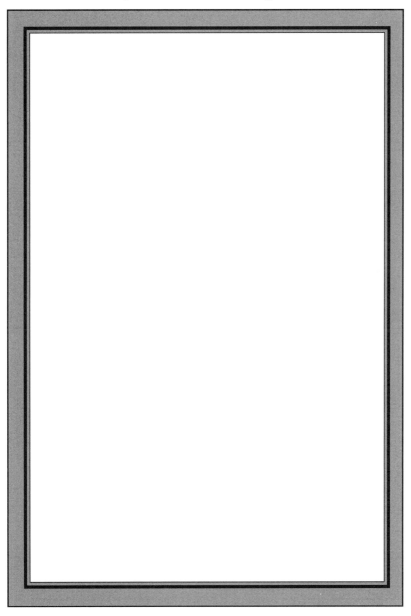

WHY AN EMPLOYER
SHOULD HIRE YOU

Use some of the words below to come up with three "super statements." Circle all the words that describe you:

Dedicated	Calm	A "doer"
Creative	Dependable	Energetic
A quick learner	Conscientious	Efficient
Success-oriented	Organized	Considerate
A hard worker	Loyal	Sensitive
Helpful	Good-natured	Dynamic
Reliable	Friendly	Open-minded
Flexible	A team player	Resourceful
Outgoing	Truthful	Assertive

> What other words can you think of
> to describe yourself?

The words you have chosen are your strengths.

Now take some of the words you found and write super statements about yourself:

Example

I AM dependable and hardworking *(strength)*.

BECAUSE when I worked with **MR. WILSON** *(whom)* at **INSTANT SHADE** *(where)* as a **CLERK** *(what)*, I received a promotion to department supervisor *(proof)*.

Super Statement 1

Strength: I AM...

Proof: BECAUSE...

Super Statement 2

Strength: I AM...

Proof: BECAUSE...

Super Statement 3

Strength: I AM...

Proof: BECAUSE...

These three statements are the top three reasons why an employer should hire you. Write them down again on this page.

LEARN THEM!
BELIEVE THEM!
BELIEVE IN YOURSELF!

```
1.




```

```
2.




```

```
3.




```

TARGETING JOBS AND EMPLOYERS

JOBS AND BUSINESSES YOU'RE INTERESTED IN

Now that you know quite a bit about your interests and strengths, you should translate them into jobs and businesses where you would be happy. List them below. They will help you decide where to apply and for what type of work.

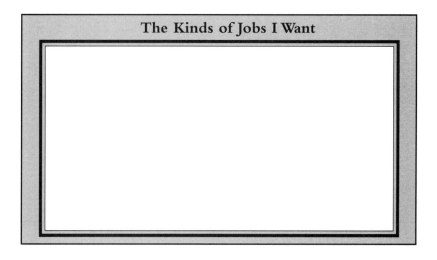

The Kinds of Jobs I Want

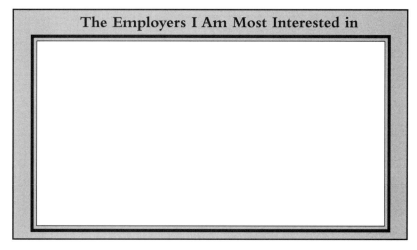

The Employers I Am Most Interested in

THE JOB MARKET

MOST JOBS ARE NOT ADVERTISED

A successful job seeker is aware that most available jobs are not advertised. These jobs are referred to as being within the "hidden job market."

A. **Employment agencies** handle 8% of available jobs.

B. **Want ads** represent 12% of all jobs.

MOST JOBS COME FROM:

C. **Friends and relatives**

D. **Employer and worker contacts**

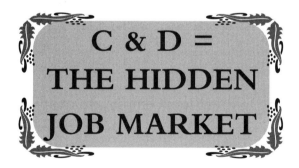

C & D =
THE HIDDEN
JOB MARKET

Getting Familiar with the Job Market

A successful job seeker realizes that it is necessary to use as many resources as possible. This is the way you will gain information about potential leads to find a job.

Advertised Job Market

✔ Review the **want ads** in the Sunday edition of your local paper, which usually contains most of the current openings.

✔ Contact **private employment agencies** and register with them.

Hidden Job Market

✔ Talk to friends and relatives.

✔ Use the **yellow pages** of the telephone book. Look under the categories that apply to you or where you would like to work.

✔ Take time to **meet local employers** near your home to become comfortable meeting employers.

✔ **NETWORK, NETWORK, NETWORK** ... ATTEMPT TO GET AT LEAST TWO NEW NAMES FROM EACH PERSON YOU CONTACT.

COMPANIES THAT
DO THE HIRING

You might wonder whether you would do better with a small company, a medium-sized company, or a large company. Look at the chart below. You will see that small companies do most of the hiring.

Companies with 1 to 20 employees

70%

Companies with 21 to 500 employees

20%

Large companies with 500+ employees

10%

Look at the next page to see the advantages and disadvantages of trying to find a job with different-sized companies.

COMPANIES WITH 1 TO 20 EMPLOYEES

✔ The smaller companies do most of the hiring.

✔ These companies are growing.

✔ Additional positions continue to develop.

✔ More opportunities to advance are offered.

COMPANIES WITH 21 TO 500 EMPLOYEES

✔ Medium companies often continue to grow.

✔ The number of employees continues to increase.

✔ Additional department heads are hired.

✔ Opportunities to advance are offered.

COMPANIES WITH 500+ EMPLOYEES

✔ The probability of growth is more limited. These companies often have to reduce their work force.

✔ When hiring is conducted, the hires are usually recruited from within.

✔ These companies have well-known names, and applicants tend to apply more readily to companies with well-known names. Competition is therefore increased.

WHAT EMPLOYERS LOOK FOR

WHY AN EMPLOYER WILL HIRE SOMEONE

There are four main factors that will persuade an employer to hire you. They are, in order of importance:

✔ PACKAGING

◆ Neat appearance

◆ Good eye contact

◆ Smile

◆ Firm handshake

✔ RESPONSIVENESS

◆ Your response to the interview questions.

◆ Positive body language.

◆ Positive attitude.

✔ EXPERIENCE

◆ Having the experience the employer wants.

✔ HAVING A CONNECTION

◆ Being recommended by an employee

◆ Knowing the person who is doing the hiring

◆ Having something in common with the employer

Think about what you can do to improve yourself in each of these factors.

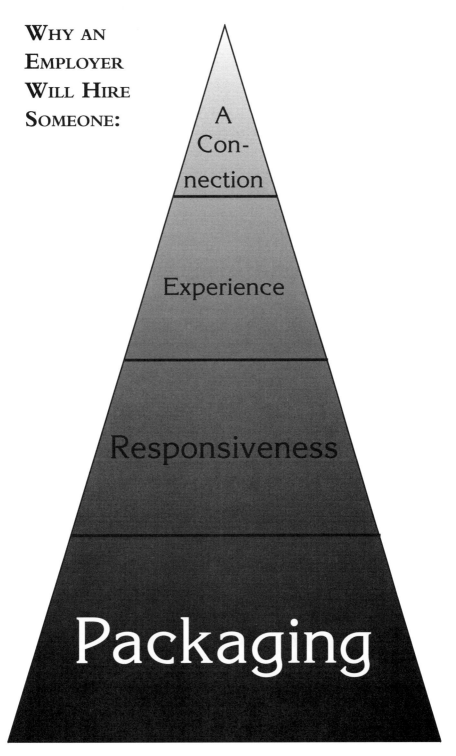

A Con- nection

Experience

Responsiveness

Packaging

YOUR APPEARANCE

PACKAGING probably ranks number one in importance to most employers. This is so important to getting the job you want!

✔ GENERAL GUIDELINES

◆ Show respect for the employer by how you dress. This will demonstrate you care about getting the job and probably will care about the quality of your work.

◆ Be sure to give yourself enough time to get ready so that you do not have to rush.

◆ Take great care about your appearance.

◆ Be sure your clothing is clean and pressed.

◆ Pay special attention to personal hygiene: bathe; use deodorant.

◆ If you have tattoos, be sure they are covered.

◆ Buy a special interview outfit and wear it only for interviews.

✔ WOMEN

◆ Wear light makeup with soft colors. Dark outlined lipstick usually is not acceptable to an employer.

◆ Manicure your fingernails.

◆ When wearing perfume, use it sparingly.

◆ Be sure your hair is one shade of color.

◆ Wear a neat hairdo. If you have long hair, wear it up away from face.

◆ Wear an appropriate dress or blouse and skirt.

✔ MEN

◆ Wear a tie and light-colored shirt or white shirt.

◆ Be sure to shave the day of the interview. However, do not shave your head as this style is often not acceptable to employers.

APPLYING
FOR JOBS

APPLYING FOR JOBS IN PERSON

Take the initiative and talk with employers directly. This is an extremely effective way of finding a job.

1. Ask for the name of the manager or the person who does the hiring and write it down.

2. Ask, "May I please speak with the (_manager/ hiring person_)."

3. Address the employer by name and introduce yourself.

4. **Ask if there is a job opening** for a _(position you want)_.

IF YES ➡ Set up an interview time.

IF NO ➡ Ask them if they know of another company that is hiring.

---

5. Say, "Thank you."

USING THE TELEPHONE

Knowing proper telephone technique and understanding the importance of the telephone will help you get a job. When you make a telephone call, your voice and speech influence the listener's impression of you. You want to give potential employers a positive impression, not only by what you say, but by how you say it.

Successful communication over the telephone is **VOCALLY EXPRESSIVE**. You can project a picture of yourself by practicing your style on the telephone. Your smile can be "heard" over the phone, so whenever you use the phone ... **SMILE!**

MAKING EMPLOYER TELEPHONE CONTACTS

◆ Introduce yourself and make sure you know who you are talking to and that you know his or her name.

◆ Be confident.

◆ Speak in short sentences.

◆ Speak slowly.

◆ Be brief. The employer may be in a hurry.

◆ Clearly explain the reason for your call.

◆ If there is something said you don't understand, ask the employer to repeat it.

◆ When unable to reach the person you need to talk to, ask when that person will be available. Be sure to call him or her back.

If you reach the right person, that is, someone who can set up an interview:

◆ **Ask if there is a job opening** for a *(position you want)*.

IF YES →	Set up an interview time.	
IF NO →	Ask them if they know of another company that is hiring.	

◆ Say, "Thank you."

Keys to Good Listening

The most important part of talking to employers, whether by phone or in person, is to listen to and understand what each person is saying. To learn what an employer is looking for, you have to be a good listener.

Here are some tips for good listening.

◆ LIMIT YOUR OWN TALKING.

◆ Ask questions.

◆ Listen for ideas ... not just words.

◆ Use brief encouragers to show you are listening. For example, you could say, "Yes,... oh,... I see."

WRITTEN
TOOLS

YOUR RESUME

Your resume is an introduction of yourself that is sent to the employer in advance or presented at the interview. It highlights your past work history, education, and objective in employment.

The resume is the employer's screening tool when more than one person is applying for a job. The employer makes a decision based on what is written, so it should be accurate, neat, and easy to read. Your resume should be written to make someone want to hire you.

Some employers in today's job market request resumes. This may include nonprofessional positions because resumes make it easier for the employer to know, at a glance, if you are the person he or she may be interested in hiring.

If you have difficulty communicating or do not speak English, the resume and cover letter are especially great tools. In many ways, they can speak for you.

> **YOUR RESUME SHOULD BE WRITTEN TO MAKE SOMEONE WANT TO HIRE YOU.**

CREATE YOUR OWN RESUME

1. Write your name, phone number, and address at the top of the page.

2. Select a work objective title. Direct it to the group of employers who hire in the area you wish to apply in. Choose a title from the list below and put the number for it in this box ☐.

   1) POSITION DESIRED

   2) JOB GOAL

   3) EMPLOYMENT OBJECTIVE

   4) CAREER OBJECTIVE

   5) JOB OBJECTIVE

   6) OBJECTIVE

   7) CAREER GOAL

   8) EMPLOYMENT TARGET

   To select a work objective summary, choose a letter from this section and put it in this box ☐.

   A. To obtain a position where I can prove my hardworking ability and contribute to the growth of the organization.

B. To work with people and contribute to the company while improving my skills.

C. To obtain a position where I can use my experience to benefit the company as well as myself.

D. To obtain a position where I can utilize my skills.

E. To obtain a people-oriented position where I can use my skills to serve others.

F. To obtain long-term employment with a company where I can contribute my hardworking ability and my positive attitude.

G. To obtain a position where I can utilize my skills and be of service to others.

H. To obtain a position where I can use my knowledge and strengths to help others achieve goals as well as myself.

I. To obtain a position where I can be challenged and develop my leadership qualities.

3. Take your objective title and summary and fill it in below your address at the top of your resume page.

Now you can introduce yourself and your abilities:

4. List your education accomplishments.

5. List your skills. (optional)

6. List your work experiences. Include the name and location of employers and how long you worked there. Describe your job duties.

7. It is a good practice to include any related volunteer work in your resume under "Related Experience." Also, list any special interests you have.

8. Write down one or two references or write "References available upon request."

RESUME SAMPLE A

JENNIFER HOPPING

1610 Orly Street   Phone: (123) 456-7890
Irvine, CA 90027   Message: (123) 456-0987

CAREER OBJECTIVE: To obtain a position where I can utilize my knowledge of marine science while contributing with genuine love to the care of sea animals.

EDUCATION:
California State University/Fullerton
Psychology Major

EXPERIENCE:
CHICKS SPORTING GOODS, Torrance, CA
Sales Associate
March, 1995 - Present
Served as a cashier, sales, customer service, and performed light clerical duties.

RAYNE WATER, Los Angeles, CA
Secretary June, 1993 - March, 1995
Established rapport with customers, conducted sales, and managed business office.

ADDITIONAL EXPERIENCE:
Volunteer for "Friends of the Sea Lions," working hands on with sick seal lions, elephant seals, and harbor seals. Provided tube feeding and hand feeding, administered IVs, maintained a clean environment.

SPECIAL SKILLS:
- SCUBA Diving (training at California State University/ Fullerton to be a dive master)
- Excellent public relations
- Experienced actress, singer, and dancer

REFERENCES: Available Upon Request.

Resume Sample B

STEVEN MORRISSEY
5772 Sutton Drive
Lawrence, KS 66047
(123) 456-7890

OBJECTIVE:
To obtain a position where I can utilize my skills and
be of service to others.

EDUCATION:
Garfield High School, Lawrence, KS
Date of Graduation: June, 1995

EXPERIENCE:
12/94 - present
Music Plus, Lawrence, KS
Sales Clerk
Job Duties: Customer service, cashier, stocking, inventory.

8/94 - 12/94
Daniel's Fruit Market, Lawrence, KS
Inventory Clerk
Job Duties: Stocking, inventory, sales orders, shipping and
receiving.

SPECIAL SKILLS:
Able to communicate at all levels.
Dedicated, goal oriented, and hardworking.

REFERENCES: Available Upon Request.

Resume Sample C

ERNEST ANTHONY CASTILLO
87 Delphin Lane
Los Angeles, CA 90062
(123) 456-7890

CAREER OBJECTIVE: To obtain a position where I can use my knowledge and strengths to help others achieve goals.

AWARDS: Army Service Medal, Daughters of The American Revolution Medal, Army Achievement Medal

SKILLS:
- Bilingual (English/Spanish)
- Proficient computer skills: Internet; WordPerfect 5.1 (Windows); Lotus 1,2,3
- Excellent interpersonal skills
- Type 65 wpm
- Positive, enthusiastic attitude

EXPERIENCE:
07/91-present U. S. Army Reserve Los Alamitos, CA
Job Duties: Inventory, shipping & handling, able to drive forklifts.

11/92-2/95   Menlo Ave. Elementary School Los Angeles, CA
Responsibilities: Help second grade students in math, reading, and language arts; supervise students during their play time.

08/94-01/95   United Education Institute Los Angeles, CA
Program Coordinator's Assistant
Responsibilities: Type test and finals using Word Perfect 5.1. File student records, type memos, update student information.

EDUCATION:
University of Southern California Los Angeles, CA
- Major: Bicultural Studies

United Education Institute Los Angeles, CA
- Diploma Received

REFERENCES: Available Upon Request.

COVER LETTER

The cover letter is sent to the employer in advance, usually with your resume, or is presented at the interview.

The cover letter is your introduction to the employer. It briefly describes your past experience and gives you an opportunity to really sell yourself. Tailor it to fit a specific job or related job opportunity.

An example of a cover letter is on the next page.

SAMPLE COVER LETTER

Tamara Grullon
456 Maplewood Terrace, Apt. 4
New Orleans, LA 70119

While I have enjoyed my past work experience and have learned a great deal, I wish to pursue a career where I can use my knowledge and experience to advance according to my abilities and effort.

As you will see from my resume, I have a background in clerical work, as well as sales. I learn things quickly and would have no problem becoming trained in the intricacies of your business. Of course, I am willing to attend whatever schools or seminars are required.

OPTIONAL PARAGRAPH: I have excellent "people skills." I can communicate effectively at any level and am able to persuade and motivate others. I work well independently or as a team member, and know when to ask for help.

OPTIONAL PARAGRAPH: I am not looking for just any job. I want a career with a future, and am willing to devote whatever time and energy are necessary to reach my goals.

A few minutes of your time would be appreciated so that we can discuss my background and ability. I am available for an interview at your convenience, and look forward to hearing from you soon.

Sincerely,

(*Your handwritten signature*
over your typewritten name)
Tamara Grullon
Enclosure: Resume

FILLING OUT AN APPLICATION

When you fill out an application, remember the employer usually sees it before he or she sees you. He or she will judge what you are like by how your application looks and the way in which it is completed. Make it neat!

◆ Print. It is neater than handwriting. Always use a black pen.

◆ Under "salary desired," write "Open" or "Negotiable."

◆ Have all necessary information with you, including your original social security card and driver's license or state identification card. Carry your completed master application, so you can copy all the information onto the blank application.

◆ Fill all blanks. If something does not apply, indicate, "N/A" (Not Applicable) or draw a line to show you did read it.

◆ Be specific about the position for which you are applying.

◆ Indicate flexibility regarding hours and shifts you are willing to work.

◆ Indicate you are available to start work "ASAP" (As Soon As Possible).

◆ Most jobs are related to other jobs. Be creative and transfer your skills or experience to fit the job for which you are applying.

◆ Give permission to contact your last employer, even if you have none.

◆ Date and sign the application.

◆ Be neat!!

MASTER APPLICATION FOR EMPLOYMENT

PERSONAL INFORMATION

DATE _____

NAME _____
       last   first   middle

SSN

ADDRESS _____
         street   city

_____
         state   zip

PHONE NUMBER _____
         home   work   message

ARE YOU LEGALLY ABLE TO WORK IN THE US? yes _____ no _____

POSITION APPLIED FOR
    When can you start? _____
    Salary desired: _____

EVER APPLIED TO THIS COMPANY BEFORE? yes _____ no _____

    where _____ when _____

REFERRED BY: _____

GENERAL

SUBJECTS OF SPECIAL STUDY OR RESEARCH WORK
_____
_____
_____

SPECIAL SKILLS
_____
_____
_____

ACTIVITIES/PUBLIC INVOLVEMENT
_____
_____

MILITARY SERVICE

_____
_____
_____

ARE YOU CURRENTLY EMPLOYED? yes ____ no ____
MAY WE CONTACT YOUR PRESENT EMPLOYER? ____ yes ____ no ____

FORMER EMPLOYERS (LAST THREE EMPLOYERS, BEGINNING WITH MOST RECENT)

_____
_____
_____

WHICH OF THESE JOBS DID YOU LIKE BEST?

_____

WHAT DID YOU LIKE MOST ABOUT THIS JOB?

_____
_____
_____

REFERENCES (THREE PERSONS NOT RELATED TO YOU, WHOM YOU HAVE KNOWN AT LEAST ONE YEAR)

_____   _____
_____

IN CASE OF EMERGENCY, NOTIFY

_____
name   address   phone no.

"I certify that all the information submitted by me on this application is true and complete, and I understand that if any false information, omissions, or misrepresentations are discovered, my application may be rejected and, if I am employed, my employment may be terminated at any time."

SIGNATURE OF APPLICANT   DATE

_____   _____

THE INTERVIEW PROCESS

What Do You Have to Lose by Going to an Interview?

At an interview, a job seeker has everything to gain and very little to lose. Employers, however, have a lot to lose. For an employer, an interview is an investment of valuable work time. Making the wrong hiring decision can cost the business lots of time and money.

*The employer needs to really get to know you in the interview so that he or she can make the right hiring decision. The employer **wants** to interview you!*

What is the purpose of the interview?

From the employer's perspective:

◆ To meet you.

◆ To determine your interpersonal skills, attitude, job skills, and interests.

◆ To clarify information from your application and resume.

From your perspective:

◆ To meet the employer.

◆ To sell yourself.

◆ To find out if you want to work for that company.

WHILE WAITING FOR THE INTERVIEW

PICTURE SUCCESS

Before entering a company office, see yourself walking in and being greeted by smiling faces. See yourself smiling back. Picture yourself being interviewed in a positive, energetic way. See yourself closing the interview positively, shaking hands, and thanking the employer.

See yourself getting the job!

ARRIVING AT THE COMPANY

Even if you have an appointment, you may have to wait to see the employer. Be patient! The interview begins the minute you arrive at the company. People will watch to see how you act while waiting. Avoid unnecessary conversations. Instead, think about how you will sell yourself and how you will calmly answer all the interview questions.

Treat the receptionist with respect. He or she may have more influence on the decision than you think.

SHOWING YOU
LIKE THE EMPLOYER

Employers hire emotionally. They hire people they like, so be likable!

Follow through with these suggestions and your chances of getting the job you want will increase....

BE LIKEABLE AT YOUR INTERVIEW

◆ Have a neat appearance. ◆ Use a firm handshake.

◆ Be responsive. ◆ Use positive body language.

◆ Have a positive attitude. ◆ Look the employer in the eye.

◆ Smile. ◆ Smile. ◆ Smile.

Tell the employer you would really like to work for the company.

OPENING THE INTERVIEW

Use the employer's name, introduce yourself, and shake hands. State the position you are applying for.

✔ Be neat in appearance; it shows you really care about making a good impression.

✔ Extend a firm handshake.

✔ Introduce yourself.

✔ Offer the application/resume.

✔ Answer the interview questions appropriately.

✔ Demonstrate a positive attitude.

✔ Present yourself with a winning smile.

✔ Make eye contact with the interviewer.

✔ Use positive body language.

THE INTERVIEW QUESTIONS

Some job seekers make the mistake of memorizing answers to interview questions. This can cause problems. At one interview, the job seeker forgot some of his lines and fumbled the entire interview.

The successful job seeker will become only *familiar* with interview questions and responses. If you become familiar, there are no lines to memorize and no mistakes to make. What is necessary is to concentrate on your presentation.

The interview questions will be your focus point. Talk to other employees first. Learn about any positive things the company offers to its employees.

Support the company's products and services. You could say, for instance, "I feel *(no one can argue with your feelings)* that my interest and dedication to learn more about this business can make a difference in the quality of your products."

Appear confident. You might say: "Sounds like I am the person for the job." Sell yourself: "I would like to get hired, because I know I can do the job, and I will do a good job."

Most people are concerned about tough interview questions. The most common interview questions are shown on the next few pages. As you will see, the responses can be SIMPLE. Read these suggestions the day of the interview. You might want to take this sheet with you to review it before you walk into the company.

Become familiar with these responses. You do not need to memorize anything. Your answers to the same questions will change each time you interview, based on how you feel and how the interviewer asks them.

IMPORTANT TO REMEMBER

◆ Negative remarks about a previous employer are not acceptable.

◆ If you cannot say something positive, think about what you liked MOST about your last job.

COMMON INTERVIEW QUESTIONS

Practice your answers to these questions by writing down what you might say at an interview:

1. *Tell me something about yourself.*

2. *Why have you been out of work?*

3. *What do you hope to be doing in five years?*

4. *If we call your last employer, what would he or she say about you?*

5. *Do you have reliable transportation? What is it?*

6. *Why do you want to work for this company?*

```
┌──────────────────────────────────────────────┐
│                                                │
│                                                │
│                                                │
│                                                │
│                                                │
└──────────────────────────────────────────────┘
```

7. *What are some of your strengths?*

```
┌──────────────────────────────────────────────┐
│                                                │
│                                                │
│                                                │
│                                                │
│                                                │
└──────────────────────────────────────────────┘
```

8. *What can you do for this company?*

```
┌──────────────────────────────────────────────┐
│                                                │
│                                                │
│                                                │
│                                                │
│                                                │
└──────────────────────────────────────────────┘
```

9. *I've interviewed people with more experience than you. Why should I hire you?*

```
┌──────────────────────────────────────────────┐
│                                                │
│                                                │
│                                                │
│                                                │
│                                                │
└──────────────────────────────────────────────┘
```

10. *What is your biggest weakness?*

```
┌──────────────────────────────────────────────┐
│                                                │
│                                                │
│                                                │
│                                                │
└──────────────────────────────────────────────┘
```

11. *What do you expect as a starting salary?*

12. *Do you have any questions for me?*

SAMPLE ANSWERS TO COMMON INTERVIEW QUESTIONS

1. *Tell me something about yourself.*

   Why is this asked? Because employers want to know if they will like you. Talk about your personal life. Include previous work experience, job-related accomplishments, and what school you graduated from or will be graduating from. You also may want to discuss summer jobs and related volunteer experience.

2. *Why have you been out of work?*

   Be creative, but honest. For example, if there is a gap in your work history, you could say you decided to work at home as a homemaker for a while, or maybe you were self-employed or spent some time furthering your training or education.

3. *What do you hope to be doing in five years?*

   Show your commitment by saying something like: "I would like to be working for you in a position of increased responsibility."

4. *If we call your last employer, what would he or she say about you?*

   Use a *super statement* with *proof.* Example: My employer would say I am <u>dependable</u> *(strength)* <u>because</u> *(proof)*...

5. *Do you have transportation?*

   "Yes, I have reliable transportation." (This includes public transportation.)

6. *Why do you want to work for this company?*

   "I would like to work for this company because this company has a reputation of being fair." Employers like hearing the word "fair" to describe their company. Or, you could talk about how the business and job matches up with your interests and skills.

7. *What are some of your strengths?*

   Discuss your strengths and use your *super statements* with *proof.* Highlight two or three, and end by saying "I think I could use my strengths to do a good job in your company."

8. *What can you do for this company?*

You can use the same kind of answer as in the previous question. Use *super statements* with *proof.* If you know some specifics about the job and company, you could mention how your strengths "will help to get done what needs to be done."

9. *I've interviewed people with more experience than you. Why should I hire you?*

"I can't speak about others, but I am dependable and I really want to work for this company."

10. *What is your biggest weakness?*

You can respond to this in two different ways:

1. Turn a **strength** into a **weakness** into a **strength**.

Example: I am always concerned about being on time (**strength**), and sometimes that can frustrate other people (**weakness**), but being on time is very important to me (**strength**).

2. Turn a **weakness** into a **strength**.

Example: Some people may think my lack of experience is a weakness (**weakness**), but I learn things very quickly (**strength**).

11. *What do you expect as a starting salary?*

"What do you pay someone with my experience?" or, "What do you usually pay someone in this position?"

12. *Do you have any questions for me?*

"What are you looking for in the person you hire for this position?

Closing the Interview

Wait for the employer to signal that the interview is over. He or she usually will say something such as, "Well, thank you for coming in..."

Look at the employer, use the employer's name, thank him or her, and leave the impression that you really want to work for him or her. Tell the employer, "I would really like to work for you."

When you get up to leave, offer to shake the hand of the person or persons who interviewed you. Smile. You could say something like "It was nice to meet you."

◆ **Use the employer's name.**

◆ **Thank the employer.**

◆ **Give a firm handshake and smile.**

Remember, it is the employer who has the most to lose. You have the most to gain.

Be prepared to tell them that you believe you are the person that has what they are looking for and that you really want to work for them!

INTERVIEW FOLLOW-UP

After the interview has taken place, contact the employer to remind him or her that you are still interested in the position.

There are three ways of following up an interview:

◆ A telephone call

◆ A return visit to the company

◆ A thank-you note

Your follow-up should be based on the "feel" of the interview:

◆ If the interviewer was very formal and serious, a thank-you letter may be appropriate.

◆ If the interviewer was very casual, you may want to call the person the next day to thank them.

Whatever type of contact you choose, do not forget to:

◆ Identify the interviewer by name.

◆ Include your name and the position for which you interviewed.

◆ Tell them you are contacting them "to find out if any decision has been made about the job."

◆ Express your thanks again to the interviewer for his or her time.

"Hi, Ms. Jenson. My name is Ronnie Stever. You interviewed me for the office job you had open. I was calling (stopping by) to see if you had made a decision about the job...

I appreciate your taking the time to talk to me about the job."

SAMPLE THANK-YOU LETTER A

Mr. Kozo Hasagawa
LIM CORPORATION
2777 Louise Drive
San Francisco, CA 94132

Dear Mr. Hasagawa:

    I appreciate the time you spent interviewing me. I am interested in the job you described and would like to become an employee of your organization.

    As we discussed during the interview, I will call you on (<u>date</u>) to discuss the possibility of employment further. If there are other questions that I may answer, please feel free to call me at (123) 456-7890. Thank you for your consideration. I am looking forward to your decision.

Sincerely,

(*Your handwritten signature over your typewritten name*)
Skylar Smith

Sample Thank-You Letter B

Ms. Regina Orlando
JACKSON PARK DEVELOPMENT COMPANY
37 B Uptown Pike
Concord, NH 03301

Dear Ms. Orlando:

I would like to express my appreciation for the time you spent interviewing me. I am interested in the job you described and would like to become an employee of your organization.

If there are other questions that I may answer, please feel free to contact me at the number listed below. Thank you for your consideration. I am looking forward to your decision.

Sincerely,

(*Your handwritten signature over your typewritten name*)
Molly Tritell

Phone Number: (123) 456-7890

FEELING GOOD ABOUT YOURSELF DURING YOUR JOB SEARCH

USE POSITIVE SELF-TALK

Sometimes when we talk to ourselves, we use negative statements, such as "I'll never get a good job," or "Who will ever hire me?"

Saying these kind of things to yourself can work against you. Instead of comforting yourself, you teach yourself to accept defeat too quickly.

Replace negative statements with positive self-talk such as, "I can be a very GOOD employee and any employer will be HAPPY to have me work for him or her." Or, try saying the following out loud:

"I will GET the job."

"I will do a GOOD job."

"I am CAPABLE."

"I am HARDWORKING."

"THE JOB I WANT HAS MY NAME ON IT!"

PICTURE YOUR SUCCESS

Famous athletes and others say one way they practice is by picturing themselves in their mind performing perfectly. A 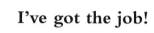 singer might "rehearse" a number in his or her imagination. Or a runner might picture winning an important race.

I've got the job!

You can use this tool, too. Have a daydream about getting a great job. Think about doing each part leading up to the interview itself.

Before entering a company office, picture yourself walking into a company and being greeted by smiling faces. See yourself smiling back.

See yourself being interviewed in a positive, energetic way. Listen to yourself as you answer questions about your skills.

As you leave, see yourself shaking hands, leaving behind you a group of happy people with smiling, shining faces and a twinkle in their eyes.

Finally, picture answering the phone and hearing those magic words: "We would like to offer you the job. When can you start?"

You Deserve a Reward

You deserve a REWARD each time you finish something that can help you land a job. For example, when you finish your resume, celebrate with a treat that you enjoy. Or when you go out looking for a job and meeting employers, end the day by doing something you like.

A reward for your efforts can be many different things. Maybe you will treat yourself to lunch, ice cream, or a movie. Or maybe you will go shopping for a special thing to wear for your next interview or the first day of your new job.

Seeing friends can be another kind of reward. Visiting with a friend after your next interview will motivate you to work even harder the next time you go out to meet employers.

Giving yourself a reward for working hard on something helps you look forward to the work. Remember, a reward should come after you accomplish something or make an effort to try something. Like jobs, we need to earn our rewards, not get them for free.

And the best reward you will get after all your efforts pay off is a new job. The little rewards you give yourself along the way will make the road to a new job easier and more fun for you.

SHARE THE EXPERIENCES OF YOUR JOB SEARCH

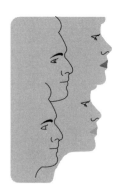

Besides being a reward, your friends are also proof that you are a WONDERFUL PERSON, the type of person people want around them. For support, choose friends with whom you can talk about your job search experience.

Concentrate on the good things that happen during the day, the positive experiences you had, and the interesting people and places you experienced. Tell your friends about these things.

Your friends probably have had similar experiences. Ask them for suggestions and job leads.

Talking about your job search to people you trust helps you stay focused on what you need to do. It also helps your friends support you when you need a boost.

IMPROVING THE CHANCES OF GETTING THE JOB YOU WANT

 Find out what makes you different and better from others who are looking for the same type of job as you! Discover what makes you stand out from the rest and be prepared to talk about it.

 Take the initiative and talk with employers directly. This is an extremely effective way of finding a job. Ask to speak to the manager, or the person who does the hiring.

 Apply to small businesses as well as large ones. Two-thirds of all of the new jobs created have been developed by businesses with twenty or fewer employees.

 Find out what type of business the companies you are applying at are in. Learn what they produce or manufacture, and the type of services they provide.

Follow up on all employer contacts, in person or by telephone.

 Describe yourself in terms of the SKILLS you have rather than in terms of the JOBS you have done.

 Include any related volunteer work in your resume as a related experience.

 Discover different names for related work in which you are interested.

 Let as many people as possible help you find a job. Tell everyone you know and meet exactly what kind of job you are looking for.

 Be well-groomed and appropriately dressed. These outward signs will help the employer and others to see that you really care about getting a job.

How to Keep Your Job Once You Get It

1. Show up.

2. Be on time.

3. Be honest.

4. Leave personal problems at home.

5. Follow the rules.

6. Work well with others.

7. Be willing to do more than asked.

8. Stay positive and be flexible.

9. Learn by your mistakes and accept criticism without resentment or excuses.

10. Take pride in the work you do.

Please remember that

no one owes you a job.

You have to sell yourself

to the employer.

Persuade through your

enthusiasm that you would

be the best person

to meet his or her needs.

*You NOW have the tools
to independently
job search.
Go for it!*

APPENDICES

PRINCIPLES OF A SELF-DIRECTED JOB SEARCH:

NOTES ON FINDING YOUR OWN JOB

◆ Treat yourself as you would your best friend who is job searching.

◆ Believe in yourself.

◆ Be confident.

◆ Be patient.

◆ Be prepared to talk about what makes you stand out from other applicants.

◆ Make a daily job-search plan.

◆ Job search for the job you really want. This will motivate you even more.

◆ Be well-groomed and appropriately dressed.

◆ Contact by phone and in person employers you would like to work for.

◆ Sell yourself to the employer.

◆ Be persuasive and congenial.

◆ Learn to deal with disappointment.

◆ Reward yourself.

◆ Share your job search experiences with positive friends for moral support.

◆ Trust your decision.

◆ The amount of time and energy you invest is exactly what you will get in return.

◆ The job you want has your name on it ... claim it!

APPENDIX 2
NOTES FOR SUCCESSFUL
JOB DEVELOPERS

Finding jobs for people can be a spiritual experience. You touch people's lives, both personally and emotionally. You can make that difference that will enable job seekers to believe they have value and can offer an employer their hardworking ability and willingness to excel.

The role of a job developer is not just getting a job for a job seeker. It's about assisting the job seeker in discovering interests and skills and becoming more self-aware through job-seeking skills. A job developer isn't just helping with job placement, but supporting a new life experience with hope for a better future.

Persuading a job seeker that a job search can be exciting and fun is possible if this is *your* mind set. A job seeker may deal with fear-based issues by displaying various behavior patterns, such as a negative attitude or indifference. To deal with this, it is important to build rapport with the job seeker. This will eventually evolve into trust, which helps allay fears. The outcome will be a job seeker who will try to succeed in his or her job search and follow-up. Listed below are guidelines for job developers to be effective.

SUCCESSFUL JOB DEVELOPMENT

◆ Accept each job seeker's personality traits and work with them unconditionally.

◆ Interact with the job seeker based on bonding, open communication, honesty, and sincerity.

◆ Establish rapport with the job seeker to build trust.

◆ Provide counseling one to one on fears the job seeker may have.

◆ Promote positive high energy.

◆ Demonstrate to the job seeker that a job search can be exciting and fun.

◆ Use creative and personalized placement to complete a successful job match.

◆ Use mood matching: Match a job seeker's personality to a specific environment or job site.

◆ Help job seekers to look outside themselves to discover their strengths and interest.

◆ Teach the dos, not the don'ts. Don't fill someone's head with unnecessary information.

◆ Job develop with one job seeker at a time. A job developer will pick up other job leads even while focusing on one job seeker.

◆ Empower the job seeker – Let each job seeker learn by doing.

◆ Canvas an area – Let the job seeker decide which employer they would like to work for.

◆ Let the job seeker know meeting employers gets a little easier each time.

◆ Motivate job seekers to participate in their job searches and to follow up on all job leads.

◆ Encourage job seekers to buddy up with a referral source or temporary agency.

◆ Be accessible to job seekers. Have them keep you up-dated.

◆ Model confidence in meeting employers.

◆ Have integrity and be fair-minded.

◆ Be patient to cope with conflicting points of view.

◆ Be prepared to deal with the unexpected and the unusual!

◆ Believe in your job seekers until they can believe in themselves. You must believe in the product you sell.

KNOWLEDGE IS POWER

Many job seekers have a limited or inaccurate knowl-edge of the labor market, especially as it exists in their community. In order to make more effective job choices, job seekers must have information on:

1. the types of jobs that exist in their communities

2. availability of job openings

3. minimum hiring requirements (education, training, work experience)

4 characteristic working conditions (physical and mental demands)

5. job accommodations

6. salary or wage levels

Self–Esteem

While teaching job-seeking skills, a job developer can work on building up the job seeker's self esteem. Your outlook is important. The job seeker will mirror your attitude. At this same time, you have the opportunity to motivate, by believing in job seekers until they believe in themselves.

Remember... employers hire emotionally. They hire people they like. Provide the job seeker with pointers on how to show they like the employer.

Preparation through job-seeking skills builds confidence. If job seekers are prepared for an interview, they will be confident and can concentrate on presenting themselves rather than worrying about the outcome.

The job developer/instructor is required to have an open heart, and the ability to accept the job seeker unconditionally, exactly the way she or he is.

ABOUT THE AUTHOR

Frances Curiel works for TransCen, Inc., where she is an employer representative in the Los Angeles, California, office of the "Bridges...from school to work" project. "Bridges" is a unique venture established and supported by the Marriott Foundation for People with Disabilities.

In addition to Marriott, Curiel has assisted numerous large and small companies in hiring, accommodating, and promoting youth with talents (who just happen to have disabilities). She has a flair and love for job development and has applied this gift for almost fifteen years in the field. She has worked for private and public rehabilitation organizations, federal and state prison systems, and JTPA programs.

ORDER FORM

Take Charge of Your Job Search!

A Handbook to Empower Unemployed People to Find Their Own Jobs

Frances Curiel

If you are looking for a job or help people get jobs, *Take Charge of Your Job Search!* is a welcome breath of fresh air. It helps unemployed job seekers who face challenges getting into the job market develop lifelong skills to find and get the jobs that are right for them.

Clear and to the point, *Take Charge of Your Job Search!* explores keys to finding your own job and what employers look for. It helps job seekers discover talents and interests, target jobs and employers, apply for jobs, and brush up on resumes and how to approach an interview.

This handy book offers sample resumes, cover letters, and thank-you notes, as well as worksheets to organize a job search.

The content can be used by job seekers themselves, or, in the case of people with significant challenges in need of support, by job developers or others who work with them. For those in this role, it offers notes on successful job development.

Take Charge of Your Job Search! prepares job candidates of varying abilities to shine for employers. ISBN 1-883302-11-0 ■ 7" x 10" ■ $20

Return form to: TRN, Inc., PO Box 439, St. Augustine, FL 32085-0439 USA.
Please make checks payable to TRN, Inc. Our EIN is 59-3215621.
All orders must include purchase order number or payment.

Phone Orders: 904-823-9800 ■ Fax Orders: 904-823-3554

Please send me _____ copies of *Take Charge of Your Job Search!* at $20 US each.

SHIPPING WITHIN UNITED STATES

$3 US for 1st book; $1 each additional book.

Contact us for shipping cost over 10 items or to other countries.

Name _____

Organization _____

Address _____

City _____

State/Province _____

Zip/Postal Code _____

Phone (_____) _____

E-Mail Address _____

■

Visit our Web site at http://www.oldcity.com/trn

or

E-mail us at trninc @aol.com